God, Money & You

60 DAYS OF FINANCIAL ANSWERS TO
CHANGE YOUR LIFE

Philip L. Liberatore, CPA

TRILOGY CHRISTIAN PUBLISHERS
TUSTIN, CA

Trilogy Christian Publishers
A Wholly Owned Subsidiary of Trinity Broadcasting Network
2442 Michelle Drive
Tustin, CA 92780

For information, address Trilogy Christian Publishing Rights Department, 2442 Michelle Drive, Tustin, Ca 92780.

Trilogy Christian Publishing/ TBN and colophon are trademarks of Trinity Broadcasting Network.

For information about special discounts for bulk purchases, please contact Trilogy Christian Publishing.

Manufactured in the United States of America

Trilogy Disclaimer: The views and content expressed in this book are those of the author and may not necessarily reflect the views and doctrine of Trilogy Christian Publishing or the Trinity Broadcasting Network.

10 9 8 7 6 5 4 3 2 1

Library of Congress Cataloging-in-Publication Data is available.
ISBN 978-1-64773-296-7
ISBN 978-1-64773-297-4 (ebook)

Contents

Dedication..v

Introduction vii

Section 1. God & Money: What the Bible Says
About Money... 1

Section 2. You & Your Money: Understanding the
Basics of Money...19

Section 3. Managing Your Money Responsibly........... 37

Section 4. Planning for the Future............................. 57

Section 5. Dealing with Financial Burdens 81

Section 6. Growing Your Business and Your
Money..101

Conclusion 125

Acknowledgements 127

Suggested Reading..129

About Liberatore Accounting Services 131

A Note From IRS Problem Solvers, Inc....................133

About *God, Money, & You*.......................................135

Endnotes 137

Contents

Dedication

This book is dedicated to the advancing of the kingdom of God by means of His Word, through the practical application of biblical principles in our lives.

Introduction

There was a season in my life when I was without a job. I had no income. I sent out approximately 600 resumes and exhausted all of my options trying to get employment.

Each day I was being forced to pull from my depleting savings. My ability to trust God was definitely being stretched. But in seeking God's direction and searching out His Word, the Lord led me to Malachi 3:10 (KJV): "'Bring the whole tithe into the storehouse, that there may be food in my house. Test me in this,' says the Lord Almighty, 'and see if I will not throw open the floodgates of heaven and pour out so much blessing that you will not have room enough for it.'"

As I read these words, the Holy Spirit began to transform my heart. Had I read this right—the Lord Almighty was asking me to test Him in the area of my money? You got it! I made the decision then that there was absolutely no way I was going to withhold my tithe from the Lord, even though I had absolutely no income. I continued to be faithful to God and continued tithing to the church 10% of what my prior income had been. For seven months I gave, and God miraculously provided for my needs. It was after those long seven months that God led me to a tax attorney who helped me to establish my own tax business. This was the beginning of a journey on which God has continued to show Himself miraculous in many ways. From the truth of Malachi 3:10 and from this excruciating yet transforming experience, God put me on a path that has led to the dream of a lifetime. In my experience, this biblical priority of giving to God first is the cornerstone principle regarding money.

Through the years, God has taken His words and has embedded them deeper into my heart. God has woven His money management principles into the fabric of my life. He continues to show me the power of consecrated giving. Every year from that time forward I have put God to the test, and it has been an incredible experience. God is faithful and true. I can guarantee you this: you can never out-give God. I challenge you to give beyond your comfort level.

Some years I have tithed based on the income I wanted to make, not on the income I was generating at the time. God blessed me in this. Within a few years, I was actually making that larger income that I had tithed on. Recently, I have given the Lord one-tenth of what I wanted to make for the year upfront—right at the beginning of January.

It has been incredible. God has given back to me time and time again, so I can financially support numerous ministries and outreach organizations. God is incredible! What an amazing opportunity we have to partner with Him. You may be asking, "Why does my money matter to God?" I am convinced that the way you manage your money plays a key role in your spiritual development and is linked to your heart transformation.

When you start giving and managing your money God's way, He will transform your life and your ability to give to others. God will bless you.

He wants to raise your standard of giving. Too many times when it comes to money we are self-focused, looking for what we can get rather than how the process of being God's steward can help conform us to the image of Christ.

This book is filled with valuable insights and financial information, all from a God-glorifying perspective. These principles have been proven in my life and in the lives of my tax and accounting clients. The 60-day journey I'm inviting you to take will change the way you think, feel, and act when it comes to money. Experiencing this paradigm shift in your relationship with money will revolutionize the way you give—and even more importantly, the way you live. You will be part of the excitement of advancing the kingdom of God. This is the heart of the matter: giving to God and being others-focused.

You may be currently hurting over money issues. Every day I speak with people who are in pain because of financial losses, economic struggles, and the relationship difficulties that often surround money. Many people find themselves wishing they could win the lottery, thinking that their money problems would go away. In reality, most of our problems have little to do with money itself. Your relationship with money can be a great source of bitterness. But if you put God first, it can be a real source of blessing. It depends on you. This book can help you to rid yourself of bad money habits and to develop new ones that will work for you. I wrote this book to help you develop a healthy, God-honoring perspective about money so that you can be free to enjoy the important people in your life.

The best answers to your toughest questions about money can't be found in the tax code. They are found in the Good Book. Along with scriptural principles, I have provided you with many practical suggestions for dealing with your money and your life. When you change your mindset about money, you can experience a brighter financial future.

God & Money: What the Bible Says About Money

"Seek first the kingdom of God"

—Matthew 6:33 ESV

In Section 1 we will take a look at what the Bible tells us about how we are to handle money, what attitude we should have toward money, and the place it has in our lives. The next ten days will start you on the right path toward handling your money from a biblical perspective.

Day 1
WHAT DOES THE BIBLE SAY ABOUT MONEY?

What does the Bible say about money? A whole bunch! Did you know that in the New Living Translation of the Bible, the word money is used eighty-four times? The word hymn is only used two times. God is definitely concerned about our attitude toward money. More specifically, He cares about our involvement with money. It matters to God:

- how we earn it,
- that we save it,
- whether we are willing to share it,
- and much, much more.

The Bible doesn't just say one thing about money; it says hundreds of things about it. God blesses people financially. (Remember the story of Abraham, when God promised to bless him and his descendants?) God also gives warnings to rich people who make money or their appetites their "gods." See the book of James, chapter one, for several examples.

Jesus' commandment to "Seek first the kingdom of God... and all these things will be added to you" (Matthew 6:33 ESV) may be the most concise summary of God's perspective on all of your needs. Put Him first, and He'll take care of the rest... including your money matters.

Day 2
ISN'T MONEY THE ROOT OF ALL EVIL?

"Money is the root of all evil" has become a famous saying, but it's not actually what the Bible states. The actual text from 1 Timothy 6:10 (NIV) reads: "For the love of money is a root of all kinds of evil. Some people, eager for money, have wandered from the faith and pierced themselves with many griefs."

Money, in and of itself, cannot be evil. It's an inanimate object! You'll never hear about a dollar bill robbing a bank. Checkbooks don't steal. It's people who can steal your checkbook. Evil is in people, not in money. It's just that money (and power, and fame, and pride, etc.) can and often does bring out the worst in us. So what the Apostle Paul is warning us about is lusting after money. Contrary to that famous scene in the movie Wall Street, greed is not good. Paul goes on to warn his young disciple, Timothy, that some people have abandoned their faith by craving money and going after it with reckless abandon. That can ruin your life. So here's the bottom line about the bottom line: money is a neutral or even good thing. But lusting after money for money's sake will lead to all sorts of evil in your life. Don't let it happen to you. Put God first.

Day 3
DOES GOD WANT ME TO HAVE MONEY?

Yes, God wants you to have what you need and then some, but He is more concerned about your heart than your bank account. God's main desire is that you put your trust in Him (not in money, your spouse, your job, or your own strength).

God does bless people financially. In fact, God is so good, "He... sends rain on the just and on the unjust" (Matthew 5:45 ESV). But He especially loves to give gifts to His children. If you have kids or grandkids, aren't you the same way? And along those lines, would you keep giving your kids gifts if they weren't grateful, didn't take care of them, or didn't share them? You'd discipline them in love so that they would learn to appreciate and share the good things you give them.

God is the same way. He doesn't need your money. He owns everything. He wants to see you dependent on Him, the source of every good gift.

Christians differ in thought about how God wants His children to prosper. My reading of the scripture teaches me that God, indeed, wants to pour out a blessing on His children—that means you. And...

- Your standard of living is already greater than any other generation that has ever lived.

GOD, MONEY & YOU

- God has blessed you with every spiritual blessing in Christ. If you are a believer, you are "in" Christ. This means that as a part of God's family, you will inherit Christ's kingdom with Him. Talk about riches!

If you want to know whether God has promised that you will be a millionaire or a billionaire, I don't think so. But God has given you biblical principles for building and sharing riches, and He will provide enough for you to fulfill your calling.

Day 4
SHOULD I GIVE TO GOD?

Many Christians believe that the idea of "tithing", or giving 10% of your income to God, is an Old Testament idea.

First, nowhere in the New Testament does Jesus or any of the apostles say to stop tithing.

Second, if you feel that this requirement has been set aside, you have to ask yourself the following question: Does God expect us to be more or less generous in the New Covenant than the Old Testament saints were in the Old Covenant?

A good rule of thumb I follow is to do both. Tithe to your local church, and give above and beyond that to Christ-centered ministries and those in need.

Tithing is a great, biblical habit you can learn. Ask people who tithe consistently if God has blessed them and their finances. Guess what? You are going to get "Yes!" answers. God guarantees it in Malachi 3:10!

Now that we've addressed whether you should give, you may wonder how much you should give. The answer might surprise you. Do you think it's 10%? 20%? Not even close. Give God all of it!

Does that mean you need to write a check to your church or a charity for all the money in your possession? Probably not. It means that God wants all of you, and that includes your money. Giving 10% of your income to God's work is a good start.

Here's a handy acronym to help you remember some of God's principles about giving. It's the word CHEER, and it reminds us that God loves a cheerful giver:

Contribute to God's work.

Happily give your tithes and offerings to God.

Equip God's people through your giving.

Evangelize with your giving to help fulfill the Great Commission.

Reach out to those in need. And don't forget to give thanks with a grateful heart.

Day 5
WHO SHOULD GET THE MONEY I GIVE TO GOD?

You should bless those who bless you. First stop: your local church. The New Testament is clear that those who spend their lives preaching the gospel should make their living from the gospel.

God is also crystal clear that we should look out for widows and orphans. Jesus's brother, James, even wrote in James 1:27 that this is "pure" religion.

Feeding the poor is not an option. We haven't been given the option of opting out of that. You can allocate some of your giving specifically to a ministry like the Salvation Army or World Vision. Or perhaps your church has specific ministries for these various areas of need.

God has not told us to "retreat." He wants to "advance" His kingdom through the Good News of the Gospel of Jesus Christ. Support mission organizations like Campus Crusade, Far East Broadcasting, The Billy Graham Evangelical Association, World Vision, and others that God may put on your heart.

When you are in doubt, do these three things:
- Pray and ask God for wisdom.
- Make sure you are involved in a Christ-honoring, Bible-believing church.

- Give to your local church. They pass the plate or offering basket each Sunday; right? Don't miss the opportunity to give!

Day 6
WHAT DOES IT MEAN TO GIVE WITH A CHEERFUL HEART?

Giving with a cheerful heart means doing so without obligation or duty! The key is not your financial position. It's the position of your heart. "God loves a cheerful giver" (2 Corinthians 9:7 ESV).

Use this acronym to help you find the cheer in your heart for giving:

Give thanks before you give anything else.

Laugh and enjoy giving to God simply because you love Him.

Accept that every good thing comes from God above and rejoice in Him.

Don't hold back. Take a look at the word "stingy." It'll sting you.

Give generously to God and to others, even when you don't feel like it. Act as if you are cheerful, and soon you will be. The point of giving is to honor and celebrate God's blessing in your own life by helping to bless others. If you do it with resentment or hesitancy, you are not showing God that you are thankful, and you are not setting the right example for others who may be watching you.

Day 7
WHAT DOES IT MEAN TO RECEIVE GOD'S BLESSINGS?

The first thing you must understand is that God blesses in many ways. He blesses us with hope in Him, with forgiveness, with life, with family and friends, and He blesses us financially. So, right off the bat, you should give thanks for the ways that God has already blessed you.

If you believe you are stuck in a spiritual rut and are not experiencing God's blessing, it is possible that God is disciplining you as His son or daughter.

This doesn't always feel good, but it's good for you. God is pruning you. He is shaping your character. God cares more about your character than He does about your bank account.

Finally, God blesses us by our obedience to His commands and laws. God's love for you will never change. He loves you with an everlasting love. But His ability to bless you comes by your obedience to His precepts. This ties into the law of sowing and reaping.

These "Three P's" will help you understand this principle:

Plant the right kinds of seeds. You will get more of whatever you sow.

Put as many seeds into the soil as you can. If you want a big harvest, you need to plant the right kinds of seeds, and plant lots of them.

Persist in planting, nurturing, and watering seeds. Imagine if a farmer planted only one or two seeds of corn, didn't see any crop, and just gave up. No. Keep planting.

As the Bible says, "In due time we will reap if we do not grow weary" (Galatians 6:9 NASB).

The final component of God's blessing is our treasure in heaven. All of life is spiritual, because we are made in God's image and we live in His creation. What Jesus said about storing up treasure in heaven is another take on the principle of sowing and reaping. When you seek first God's kingdom (Matthew 6:33 ESV), give to God's work and His people, and spread the Good News of the Gospel, you may not always see an earthly return on that investment, but you will see a return. The Bible says that God is not mocked, and "Whatever one sows, that will he also reap" (Galatians 6:7 ESV). So if you sow these good things on earth, you will reap rewards in heaven. I'll see you there. It's going to be great!

Keep an eternal perspective! (It's okay to be on the receiving end when you are in need!)

Day 8
IS GAMBLING A SIN?

A lot of people struggle with wondering if gambling is a sin. My bet is that it is. (Sorry, I couldn't avoid that pun.) Good Christians differ in opinion on this one, too. I love what Steve Allen once wrote: "I used to make mental bets. That's how I lost my mind."

The only places where the Bible talks about gambling are historical incidents; for example, when the Roman soldiers gambled for Jesus' clothing. But there are biblical principles to remember here:

- Your life is not your own; it belongs to the Lord. This means that your money belongs to God. Gambling certainly does not provide a good return on God's money.

- Gambling has become an epidemic addiction in our culture. Television shows and movies glorify it, but what they don't show you are the ruined lives, destroyed marriages, crushed hopes, and criminal records that so often accompany the gambling lifestyle.

- Set a godly example for others. Be careful about what you are modeling. The world is watching.

- The Bible says, "Whatever is not from faith is sin" (Romans 14:23 NASB). So if your conscience bothers you when it comes to the idea of gambling, don't do it!

By the way, who said that poker was a sport? If you have a gambling problem, get help. Visit *www.GamblersAnonymous.org.*

Day 9
IS BEING IN DEBT A SIN?

God's Word says, "Owe nothing to anyone except to love one another" (Romans 13:8 NASB). That is a pretty clear statement about what God thinks about debt. But please remember a couple of things here:

- God has a perfect standard, and we are not perfect.
- God forgives, and if you have put your trust in His Son, He has already forgiven you.

Also, in our culture, which is a credit-based culture, there are certain things like home ownership that make a lot of sense to buy on credit. This is because, generally speaking, your house will appreciate in value at a greater rate than you will pay in interest on your loan.

Some Christians would say that you should never go into debt for any reason, ever. I think that although that is the best rule of thumb, there are some legitimate exceptions. Home ownership is one. Family or medical emergencies are another.

Please keep in mind that our ultimate debt, the price we deserve to pay because of sin, has been paid in full. We were spiritually bankrupt, but Jesus has released us from our debt. Thank God.

Day 10
WHAT IS THE BOTTOM LINE ABOUT MONEY?

You will notice that my answers throughout this book have been based on God's wisdom, and not just on my experience as a CPA. The parable of the talents found in Matthew 25:14-30 tells of three servants who were each entrusted with talents of money: One was given five talents, another was given two talents, and the last was given one talent, each according to his ability. The story goes on to tell how the servants with five talents and two talents both doubled their talents by their willingness to take what was entrusted to them and multiply it to please their master; to each of whom the master replied, "Well done, good and faithful servant! You have been faithful with a few things; I will put you in charge of many things" (Matthew 25:21 NIV). The servant who received one talent went and buried it because he was afraid of losing it. He wasn't willing to give from what had been given to him, and the master was very displeased.

As a daily reminder of this parable, I placed in my office lobby three pictures that represent the parable of the talents (which a dear client who is an art professor from Azusa Pacific University painted). All three pictures are of a painter's canvas. The first displays one color, and the rest of the canvas is only black and white.

The second picture has five colors that the painter multiplied into ten color hues, making a lovely scene. The last picture uses ten colors that were multiplied into twenty color hues, portraying a wonderful, living picture of life. My prayer for you is that this last picture is the color of your life.

Bottom line: Give generously and use responsibly what God has given you, and God will multiply it more than you can imagine so that you can give back to Him again and again. Live your life for God, always putting Him first and always giving back abundantly to His kingdom in order to please Him and to do His will. He has proven Himself faithful. He has done it for me. He can do it for you.

You & Your Money: Understanding the Basics of Money

"Money makes a wonderful servant, but a terrible master."

– P.T Barnum

In Section 2 we will cover some of the basics of the role money plays in your life so you can avoid mistakes in the future and correct the mistakes of the past. The next ten days will build a strong foundation for you to build your financial future on.

Day 11
WHAT IS MONEY?

If you asked a hundred people what money is, you'd likely get a hundred different answers. But I think it boils down to this: Money is what you get in exchange for what you give.

This is a helpful definition because it puts the focus on what you can do to bring value to others. Earl Nightingale once said, "No man can get rich himself unless he enriches others."[1] Take the mystery out of money in your life (or the lack of money). You will have more when you serve more. One of the economic principles that the Western world is founded on is the law of supply and demand. But this might be better described as demand and supply.

Money is what is given to you for supplying what other people demand, want, or need. If what you have to offer is in high demand, your income will be high. If you increase your value, you will increase your income.

Once you have established this relationship with money, it changes the role that money plays in your life and in your relationship with God.

Day 12
WHAT SHOULD MY ATTITUDE
TOWARD MONEY BE?

Money is important. But it is not all-important. And if you are poor, don't you dare fall into the trap of thinking that if you were rich, you wouldn't have to worry about money. Many poor people idolize money more than the rich do. And, on the flip side, if you have wealth, don't buy into the mistaken idea that if you had less, you'd worry about it less.

It's not the money itself that is important. It wouldn't matter if people were exchanging seashells, feathers, or rocks. What matters to God is how we honor Him and how we love others.

Jesus, Himself, made more statements concerning money than He did about anything else. Most importantly, He said, "Do not worry" (Matthew 6:25 NIV). That means that worrying about money (or anything else) is a sin. Let me repeat that: Worrying about money is a sin. Why is that so? Because you can't worry about something and have faith at the same time. And the Bible says in Romans 14:23 NASB, "Whatever is not from faith is sin."

So then, put on an attitude of gratitude for what you have. That's called contentment. Never allow money to rule your life. But at the same time, make sure that you observe God's principles regarding money. And give thanks to God for what He has already blessed you with and what He will bless you with in the future. Praise God from whom all blessings flow.

Day 13
WHAT DOES IT MEAN TO BE A GOOD "MANAGER" OF MONEY?

Well, right off the bat, think about what the word manager means. In cases such as with a business, the manager is not the owner. That's the situation here. It's God's money. In fact, everything belongs to God (Psalm 24:1). He has given you the role of manager. And it's an important role.

Have you had the opportunity to house sit for a friend or neighbor? It's a pretty good deal. You get the use of their nice house for a week or so. But if you are a good house sitter, you do a few nice things while the owner has given you the use of the house. You might do some extra watering, some gardening, do a few dishes, take care of a repair—you know what I mean.

Jesus tells us to "occupy till I come" (Luke 19:13 KJB). (Notice that He didn't say, "Be preoccupied with money when I come.") We don't know the day when the owner will return. But we want to have His house in order. So here are some more practical ideas:
- Remember that God is the owner of your money.
- Act like it! Take good care of what He has entrusted to you.
- Honor Him when He returns by how well you have taken care of His money through giving,

investing, and blessing others with what He has freely shared with you.

Day 14
WHAT ARE THE BIGGEST MISTAKES PEOPLE MAKE WITH MONEY?

In my thirty-plus years of experience as a CPA and an IRS problem solver, I have counseled people through nearly every imaginable money mistake. Here is my top ten list of the most common mistakes (in no particular order):

- People have no idea how much money they actually make or how much they are spending.
- Most folks have no budget.
- Most men and women do not give. They do not abide by God's law of sowing and reaping. Americans spend more on dog food each year than we do on giving to worthy causes!
- The majority of people have no financial plan in writing.
- Too many people get into trouble with their tax situation or are paying too much in taxes.
- Most people are not maximizing their ability to earn money. They are focused on what they can get from work instead of what they can contribute. You'll make more when you contribute more value.

- There is too much debt, debt, debt. It's sad, but millions of us are robbing our futures to pay for our past.
- Too many people neglect saving.
- Most people buy the wrong things, and worse, buy into the wrong ideas. You know, ideas have consequences. When you buy into materialism, for example (and we sure have), you end up with quick thrills, big bills, and your soul unfilled.
- There is a fear of success. You read that right. Sure, we fear failure. But many people are afraid to take the chance to live their dreams.

Day 15
IS IT WRONG TO ACCEPT WELFARE
OR OTHER AID?

This book talks a lot about giving to those in need. It's also okay to be on the receiving end when you are in need. In fact, God is glorified when we receive and give thanks. Jesus said that our Father in heaven loves to give us gifts. Understand something here: those gifts may come from and through other people.

As far as government programs are concerned, you paid into them, so it's okay to get paid from them. Just be careful not to catch the disease of "working the system" that some people have. It amazes me how creative and hard-working some people can be when it comes to getting payouts from the government. If they thought and worked that hard at a job, imagine how successful they could be.

God's Word commands us to bear one another's burdens. But it also says, "The one who is unwilling to work shall not eat" (2 Thessalonians 3:10 NIV). There's an old Jewish saying that some people need to hear at times: "If you are looking for a helping hand, there's one at the end of your arm."

However, if you are hurting, it is a good thing to receive the gifts, ministering help, and support of others. Be sure to give thanks to God.

Day 16

IS IT A GOOD IDEA TO BORROW OR LEND MONEY?

You've heard that old expression, "Neither a borrower, nor a lender be." That's incorrect. You want to be a lender. On an investment level, when you buy mutual funds or invest in the stock market, you are lending. And if you invest wisely, you will usually get a good return.

On a personal level, God commands us to give to those in need, but never loan money you can't afford to lose. Here's why: many times, you will lose it. A loan is not a boomerang; it may not come back to you.

This is one of the reasons credit card companies charge such exorbitant interest rates. You are paying for all of the other guys who neglect to pay.

My advice is to make these loans out of your giving budget. Don't think of a loan as a financial investment. Think of it as a personal investment in someone's life.

If you must make a loan and need to get repaid, I recommend two things:

- Put your loan in writing. Be very clear about the specifics. How much money was loaned? When is it due? To whom is it payable? What happens if the money is paid back late? Is there interest on the loan?

- Have your loan paper signed by both parties as an agreement, and have it notarized. Make sure that you keep a copy in case you end up in small claims court (not good) or mediation (better).

If you find yourself on the other side and need to borrow, the following rules are good to keep in mind:

- Don't borrow more than you need.
- Try to avoid using credit cards when you borrow. The rates are worse than loan shark rates. (Avoid loan sharks too.)
- Borrow in emergencies if you must.
- Borrow when you can use the money wisely, with a clear-cut vision for growing the funds. For example, we borrow when we take out a home loan (but isn't it interesting that the original meaning of the root word "mort" in mortgage is death!).

Day 17
SHOULD I LEND MONEY TO
FAMILY OR FRIENDS?

You are commanded to be generous to those in need (Matthew 5:42); but, as I mentioned earlier, do not expect to be paid back. Kiss the money goodbye in your heart. Expectations are planned disappointments. And use funds, if you have them, from your giving budget for this. Do not take from your savings or from your family budget.

Many people say that you should never lend money to family or friends. Why do they say that? Because borrowing and lending can certainly strain relationships. That's why I believe it's best not to expect repayment. Don't tell the borrower that, but tell yourself that. It will be good for the borrower to pay you back—and that money should go right back into your giving budget to bless someone else.

That said, I do have a word of caution for you: think very wisely about giving to friends or family members who have unhealthy money-spending behaviors; be willing to lovingly say no to giving them money. You can offer to help them in other ways and direct them to places of intervention, such as debtorsanonymous. com, etc.

Day 18
SHOULD I CHANGE EVERYTHING
I AM DOING FINANCIALLY?

When people go through a book like this or feel frustration in their financial situations, they often think that they need a whole new plan. But that's not necessary. First, don't change the things that are working. If you have a good job, a good savings plan, and a habit of giving, those are good things. Increase those things. And for the things that aren't working, take them one at a time. Trying to change too much at once sets you up for failure.

Where should you start? Well, you can begin by answering this question and taking action on it: What one change could you make that would give you and your family the best immediate return?

For example:

- Start something beneficial, such as giving to your church, opening an IRA account, or sending a "thank you" to your customers.
- Stop something that is hurting you, such as giving up drinking (with God's help), saying goodbye to gambling, or not eating out every day for lunch.

You will feel overwhelmed if you try to make too many changes too soon. Choose the one or two that will give you (and those around you) the biggest lift. Commit to those changes and see the difference in your life.

Day 19
HOW CAN I AVOID COSTLY LIFE EVENTS?

There are numerous things that happen in life that we can't predict or prepare for emotionally. The only way to be prepared for them financially is by reducing debt, increasing saving, and maintaining our giving to honor God.

There are events such as the birth of a child or college expenses that you can plan for, and then there are things such as divorce that you can plan to avoid. One of the first things that you can do is to take the word *divorce* out of your vocabulary. In certain circumstances (e.g., adultery), you are on biblical grounds for divorce. But even then, as God has forgiven you, you can ask Him to help you forgive your spouse. (Note: I am not suggesting that you should ever live with or tolerate abuse or allow your children to be abused in any way. Report it and stop it immediately.)

Below are some ways to "divorce-proof " your marriage:

- Put God first and your spouse second in all things (even before your kids—the best way you can love them is by modeling a successful marriage).
- Never become emotionally or physically intimate with someone of the opposite sex apart from your husband or wife.

- Have a regular "just us" time, date night, and getaway weekends.
- Do not separate from each other except for times of prayer and fasting.

If, God forbid, you find yourself in a divorce situation, try to de-escalate the drama. Those arguments and exchanges help nobody but the lawyers who are billing you and your "ex" on an hourly basis. Try to settle things through a mediator, and keep your heart open to reconciliation. Divorce is costly on many levels, and it is one life event that is possible to avoid.

Day 20
WHAT DO WEALTHY PEOPLE
KNOW THAT I DON'T?

There seems to be such a great divide between the "haves" and the "have-nots" that it can make those who are struggling financially wonder, *What do they know that I don't?*

Not as much as you might imagine. Usually wealthy people, especially those who have earned their way into the money, know a couple of critical things about money. And, more importantly, they act on them.

1. It's all about basic math. Cut your expenses and increase your income. Don't spend more than you make. I know that can sound so much easier said than done, but it's really that simple.

2. Compound interest can make an enormous difference in how your money works for you. (We will get into that more later.)

The main difference between you and a wealthy person is not in what they know; it's in what they do. Have you ever walked down the aisle of a retail store, noticed some new product, and thought to yourself, *Hey, I had an idea for that!* The person who got their product on the shelf took their idea and acted on it. You can do that too.

Managing Your Money Responsibly

"I have enough money to last me the rest of my life—unless I buy something."

– Jackie Mason

In Section 3 we will look at how to make good choices in the many ways you will use your money. You will learn the basics of budgeting and developing good spending habits, as well as the principles behind making good money decisions on your own.

Day 21
HOW CAN I DEVELOP GOOD MONEY HABITS?

The natural thought process when considering money is to figure out how to make more and keep it. Let's start by defining specifically what good money habits are:

- the habit of giving from the heart,
- the habit of saving systematically,
- the habit of sowing and reaping on purpose.

Based on my understanding and experience of scriptural principles, I believe that the first imperative is to give more. With these principles in mind, it is important to make them a consistent part of your life—a habit.

There is only one way to create strong habits in any area of your life, including managing your money: *repetition*. Give each week. Save each week. Sow seeds in good soil each week. Experts in human behavior have pointed out that it usually takes twenty-one days to incorporate a new habit into your life. Avoid the trap of trying to learn too many new habits all at once.

As you go through this book, highlight some of the principles and suggestions that seem especially relevant to your life, pick the top three, and narrow those down to what you think you should start with first. Make that one thing a habit for a month, and then move down the list to number two and number three. Determine your habits carefully, because they will end up making (or breaking) you. You can earn God's way—through serving others. You can save and invest the money God has generously given to you. And, perhaps most importantly, you can give to God's work, His people, and those in need.

Next, understand that just as "your life is not your own," neither is your money. God has entrusted you with it. He wants to see if you will be faithful to Him with your finances. Remember the words of Jesus:

"Whoever sows sparingly will also reap sparingly, and whoever sows generously will also reap generously. Each of you should give what you have decided in your heart to give, not reluctantly or under compulsion, for God loves a cheerful giver. And God is able to bless you abundantly, so that in all things at all times, having all that you need, you will abound in every good work" (2 Corinthians 9:6-8 NIV).

Be faithful with what you've got. Share it! Give it to God's work. You'll be blessed for it.

Day 22
WHAT ARE THE THREE BIGGEST
MONEY WASTERS?

It's going to be hard to just name three money wasters, but I'll give it my best shot. Ask yourself these questions:

- Do you waste money by using credit cards and not paying off the balance each month? Right there you are throwing hundreds, maybe thousands of dollars away with those giant monthly interest payments.

- Do you buy new at top dollar, when you could buy used or generic for far less? This category can cover everything from cars to vitamins.

- Do you pour money into liabilities or assets? Most people waste money on things that are liabilities. Author Robert Kiyosaki says, "A liability eats you; an asset feeds you."[2] Things like new furniture, DVDs, unplanned vacations, impulse shopping—these things eat you. They don't last, and they give you no return on your money.

These are general categories. The specific wasters are numberless. Maybe you spend too much on music, coffee, or new clothes. Take a hard look at each category and your spending habits. Look for ways to spend more! That's right! But spend more on the right things, i.e., giving, serving, marketing your business, your kid's education, your church, your savings, and your investments. Spending doesn't have to be a waste if it is directed at the right things.

Day 23
HOW CAN I SPEND LESS THAN I EARN?

When it comes to spending less, this acronym might help you:

Lower your wants. (And don't confuse your wants with your real needs.)

Enlist your family. Ask them to join you on a debt-reduction and super-savings plan. Make it fun, and see how good it feels to have money to give.

Shop on a full stomach. This means: don't go to the grocery store when you're hungry. And don't go shopping for clothes just because you are hungry for something new. Budget before you buy.

Seek out bargains. For example, did you know that you can save an average of 15% to 40% by buying generic brands? You can go to a "dress for less" store and often get the same name brands at a fraction of the cost. Make shopping something you do to get what you need, not something you do to fill an emotional need.

Monthly budgets are one of the biggest challenges people face. It can be really hard to set one that is realistic, and even harder to stick to it. The first thing is to be honest—brutally honest—with yourself and your spouse. Now, here's an exercise to help you lower your expenses:

1. Make a careful list of all of your monthly expenses.

2. Total them up.

3. Eliminate 20% of the money total. For example, if your monthly expenses are $10,000, take $2,000 off.

4. Go back and refigure your true, hard expenses and budget in such a way that you pay for those products and services for $8,000 per month instead of $10,000. If you can't get those items for less, begin cutting out or cutting down the things that are not necessities (clothes, bowling, movies, etc.).

5. Now, if you really need to, you can put back 10% of the money; in this case, $1,000. You may find that you can get by without putting it back. Most people can get by on 80% of their income. But you can take the 10% and reinsert it if you feel you must. This way, you still have cut your monthly expenses/budget down by 10%.

By spending less than you earn, you will truly experience how less can be more in your life. You will have more savings, more to give, and more fulfillment in your life.

Day 24
I AM HAVING TROUBLE MAKING ENDS MEET.
WHAT SHOULD I DO?

When you find yourself worrying about making ends meet, stop focusing on money or your lack of it. Instead, get very focused on what you do best when it comes to work. Get good rest and get to work! Ask your friends, family, and church body to help lift you up emotionally and to help take care of your family temporarily, if necessary.

You have to take care of your health and wellbeing. Cut out every negative influence in your life as much as you can. Stop watching TV. Don't hang around complainers. Do all that you can to create income, and ask your creditors to give you extra time to pay them. If possible, create a repayment plan that you can live with. Probably the greatest mistake that people make in times of financial problems is to stop tithing. I have spoken to countless people who naturally think this is an area that can be cut. There is nothing further from the truth. It is during these times that God desires to grow our faith and dependence on Him. During these times, we have the opportunity to experience the truth of God's principles first hand. First things first. Be certain that you continue to give God the first fruits of your labor, and use the rest responsibly.

Day 25
HOW CAN I WORK WITH MY SPOUSE TO SOLVE MY FINANCIAL PROBLEMS?

You and your spouse are a team in all areas of life, and your financial situation is one of the most important for working together. But it is important to approach this in a very careful and loving manner.

More than likely, one spouse will take the lead on handling the finances, paying the bills, monitoring the bank accounts, etc. The key to working together is to always be in communication on financial decisions. Maybe you've heard it said that you shouldn't use words like "never" and "always" in communication. Perhaps this is where the exception lies. Develop a shared vision and always be in agreement; never make financial decisions without communicating with your spouse.

Remember that God has put your partner into your life to teach you to be holy. Holiness is more important to God than happiness— happiness follows holiness. Here are seven things to agree upon together:

- financial goals
- a budget
- giving goals
- a savings and investment plan
- education for your children
- home ownership

- life insurance and a will

These are the most important areas to discuss, but the most vital word is the word "together". Staying together and working together is more important than having your way about the budget. Serve one another, and do all that you can to communicate (even if you need a counselor or pastor to help). Develop a shared vision.

Day 26
SHOULD I BUY A HOUSE OR RENT?

Choosing where to live is a big decision. Equally important is the choice to rent or to buy. The first question to ask is: Which is wiser for you at this time?

Long term, owning a home is wise because home values generally appreciate faster than the interest rate that you are paying. However, God might be calling you to the mission field or to another opportunity, so it would be smarter for you to use your "seed money" to pursue what God has equipped you to build. It might be better to rent temporarily and buy later. Most people don't own their homes anyway—the bank does. The secret is to seek God's will, to follow His principles for giving and saving, and then to decide accordingly.

Owning a home may be the American Dream, but it may not be your dream, and it may not be God's plan for you or be right for His timing. My wife and I have owned two homes in the twenty-six- year span of our marriage. In each purchase, we waited on the Lord's timing. We prayed and fasted and asked God to confirm the purchases to us in very specific ways. There were several homes we pursued, but the Lord was faithful to answer our prayers and close those opportunities and to open the purchases He guided us to make. Ask Him! He will definitely show you!

Day 27
IS IT BETTER TO BUY A NEW CAR OR A USED ONE?

Everyone loves that "new-car smell," but buying a brand-new car rarely makes sense. It's almost always better to buy a used car, for the following reasons:

- As soon as you drive off the lot, a new car goes down in value by thousands of dollars. That's an expensive first drive.
- Cars, unlike homes in most cases, do not appreciate in value, so think of your car as an expense, not an investment.
- With a good warranty and service plan, a two-year-old car will look, drive, and operate like new.

And please remember, just as with buying a house, when you buy a car you are also purchasing the loan you get. Make sure it's one you can live with. Better yet, pay cash for your car. This also will help you to negotiate a lower price.

When it comes to buying a car, keep in mind that your best negotiating advantage is your willingness to walk right off the dealership lot. Don't ever get pressured into buying a vehicle that you don't need or can't afford.

Day 28
HOW MUCH MONEY SHOULD I GIVE TO MY KIDS?

When it comes to money and teaching your kids how to be wise with it, the sooner they earn it, the better they learn it.

My wife and I have two wonderful daughters. Our perspective is that their allowance is theirs, just because we love them. It is a reasonable, modest amount. Extra money can be earned by doing odd jobs like babysitting or extra chores around the house.

There is no set amount that you should or should not give to your kids. The key is to remember that, just like your money, your kids don't really belong to you—they belong to God. Your job is to help them to become dependent on God and not on you. You will do this primarily by your example. They won't always listen to what you say, but they will watch what you do; so make sure that you are plugged into a local church and supporting the ministry with your time, talents, and giving.

Most importantly, teach your children to tithe. When our daughters started getting an allowance, we ordered personal tithe envelopes from our church with their own tithe number. Weekly, we taught them to set aside 10% of their allowance for tithe, 5% for church offering, 10% for giving gifts to family and friends, and 10% to a savings account. We encouraged them to use the other

65% to save up for something they really wanted to purchase, or to use it as they chose. In this way, they were able to have the joy of placing their tithe and offering into the offering plate and to experience worship in giving. They were also able to experience the gratification of opening up a savings account and making deposits periodically. They also knew that when they gave gifts to others it was truly coming from their hearts, because it came from their own pocket book. We feel that this was great preparation for developing godly stewardship of money in their lives.

Day 29
SHOULD I SEND MY KIDS TO PRIVATE CHRISTIAN SCHOOLS?

You need to think and pray this through with your spouse. Here's what is most important: God has given you, as the parent, the responsibility of raising and training (and that includes educating) your children. From the time they start kindergarten all the way through college, you will have decisions to make regarding their education. You may wonder about whether you should use public, private, or religious-based schools. Nowhere in the Bible is the state or the church given this commandment.

There are godly people with kids who are home-schooled, who go to private Christian schools, and who go to public schools. The key is for you to understand that whoever you allow to educate your kids is your responsibility. If you, like most of us, can't do the home-school route, you will be delegating this responsibility to others. That's okay. Delegating is a good thing. Just be wise about it.

And remember, you cannot educate kids in a moral vacuum. It's impossible. There really is no neutrality when it comes to values. Personally, my kids have blossomed within the setting of Christian education. If I had to choose between a smaller house and having my kids go to a Christ-honoring school, guess what? We're moving to a smaller house. But you need to make this decision prayerfully.

Once they are looking to college, you will be even more attuned to the financial component of educating your kids. Will you get loans, scholarships, require your kids to do work study? A better question might be, "Is college a good thing for my child?" And, if so, which colleges are the best? Much of this depends on your college student. (Or, if you are a college student reading this book— and I commend you—it depends on your unique situation.) If you decide to pay your son or daughter's way, I highly recommend that you hold them accountable for a solid grade-point average.

Regarding loans, the rates on student loans are very competitive. If you look at college as a necessary or strategic investment, you could justify taking out a college loan. For example, going to law school and paying for it with student loans might be justifiable if you are confident that you can get a good return on that investment when you pass the bar and begin billing clients as an attorney.

Make sure that your college student pays their own way as much as possible, whether through scholarships, paid internships, part-time work, or full-time work in the summer. This will give your student critical life experience and will help him or her to value their education. As a family, you have a vested interest in making the best and most responsible choices about education. Work together to decide what is right for you.

Day 30
WHAT ARE THE CATEGORIES THAT
MAKE UP A BUDGET?

Budgets are critical to financial success, no matter how large or small your income. Here's a basic sample budget for personal finances:

- Housing
- Utilities
- Home and cell phones
- TV/Cable
- Transportation
- Food
- Personal insurance and pensions
- Personal taxes
- Computer and internet
- Entertainment
- Apparel and products and services
- Health care
- Miscellaneous expenses
- Education
- Personal care products and services
- Cash contributions
- Church giving
- Books
- Savings
- Giving Fund
- Total

The most important thing is not which type of budget you use; the key is that you use one. Find one that works and start working it. You'll be so glad that you did.

Planning for the Future

"There once was a very cautious man, who never laughed or cried. He never cared; he never dared; he never dreamed or tried. And when one day he passed away, his insurance was denied. For since he never really lived, they claimed he never died."

—Anonymous

Section 4 is an important part of your financial life. It is important to be a good steward of what God blesses you with beyond just using your money responsibly. You also need to learn how to make your money work for you.

Day 31
WHAT DO I NEED TO KNOW ABOUT SAVING MONEY?

The why is the first question to answer about saving. Jesus told us to be busy about His business and to leave the rest in His hands. God has called you to be faithful to Him, and we don't know whether the earth will be here just a few more days or for hundreds and hundreds of years to come.

Some people may use the end of the world as a handy excuse for them to not be faithful to the assignment that God has given them to glorify Him. You might say, "Why polish the brass on a sinking ship?" But Jesus said, "The gates of hell will not prevail against my church", so let's get going. Make a difference. Give money. Make money. Save money.

It is irresponsible not to plan financially as though you will live until you are 100. Just plan spiritually as though you will go to your real home tonight!

Because Jesus said, "For where your treasure is, there your heart will be also" (Matthew 6:21 ESV).

The best way to save money is to start today. There is no one special way, but understanding the importance of saving in being a good manager of God's money is important.

Like a good farmer, you want to see a healthy harvest. Hiding money in your pillowcase or under your bed is one form of saving, and it certainly beats blowing your money on lottery tickets. But there are better ways to get a return on what God has entrusted to you.

A good, basic savings account at your bank that yields a small percentage of interest is a decent way to start. Other ways that yield a higher rate of return are:

- mutual funds
- stocks and bonds
- treasury bills
- real estate investments

Note: Life insurance, though highly recommended as a way to protect your family, is not a good investment or savings tool. I think that you should avoid whole life insurance, and buy term life insurance instead. A couple of decades ago, A.L. Williams turned the insurance world upside down with a great slogan: "Buy term (life insurance) and invest the difference." Take the difference in cost and save or invest it.

More important than where you put your savings is how you save. Save regularly, and save systematically (the same time, the same way, every month). The biggest take-away is just to be sure to make saving as much a part of your financial plan as paying the utility bills.

Day 32
HOW MUCH SHOULD I SAVE?

You should save a minimum of 10% of your income. That's a minimum. How can you do that? Here is the secret: Make more and spend less.

Finding that 10% for your savings is not as hard to do as you might imagine. For example, if you can make just 5% more each year (through raises, bonuses, side jobs, consulting, etc.) and spend just 5% less (eating out less often, cutting out soft drinks, buying less merchandise, etc.) you will have that 10% and you'll hardly even feel it.

In terms of an emergency savings account, ideally you want to have one year's worth of income in savings. This should be in a liquid (meaning you can access the cash) savings account. Most people don't have that much saved, but work toward having a minimum of three months' salary saved. This will give you the freedom to look for another job if you need to. Or, if you get laid off (and this does happen), you won't panic.

Plan, so you don't have to live paycheck to paycheck. That's not being wise with your income. Even the small creatures that we share this earth with store up food for the winter season, so set aside at least three months' worth of money in your emergency savings account.

Once you have this minimum covered, you can start saving toward bigger, future life events and needs. One example of this is planning ahead for marriage and family.

In Biblical times, men took a year off of work to tend to (and adjust to) their new brides. Guess what that means? They had at least a year's worth of savings to live on! [A side note: Your wedding is an important day, but don't spend so much on that one day that you put yourself (or your parents) behind for years. It's just not worth it. Make it a wonderful celebration, not a status event.]

Keep in mind that as a couple, you may be in a better place financially than you were as singles. You share living expenses, meals, travel costs, and more.

If you have found the right person, and they are ready to share your life in God, don't let the lack of money hold you back. Warning: The most important thing that you can do for your financial future is to make sure that you are on the same page with the person you plan to marry on money matters. If you are already married, make sure you get in alignment before you have kids or before you make any more big decisions that will affect your financial future and your relationship.

Day 33
HOW DO I DECIDE ABOUT CHARITABLE GIVING?

Here is an important principle: Don't just give where you feel the need; give where you believe God has called you to give. Even Jesus did not heal everybody in Israel. He was called to minister to certain people, and He faithfully did just that. You have been called, too.

There are three keys to knowing how to choose:

- Where has God placed you?
- What has God placed on your heart?
- Who has God put in your path?

There are no accidents or coincidences with God. When you ask Him to direct your steps, He will lead you to the ministries and ministers He has called you to support.

Every Christian is commanded to support the Great Commission of spreading the Gospel of Jesus Christ around the world. If you can't physically "go" into all the world, you can still help spread the Good News by supporting Christian missionaries. Here are a few guidelines:

- Make sure that the missionaries you support are spreading the real Gospel (1 Corinthians 15:1-5).

- Make an effort to support the missionaries your local church is sponsoring. They are an extended part of your church family.
- Make a strong attempt to do some missions work yourself. Can't make it to Africa for ten years? How about going to Mexico for two weeks next summer? You don't speak Indonesian? Okay. How about working with your inner city mission in the town where you live?

In fact, it is okay to give to more than one ministry; so you can do more than one or all of these.

In a certain sense, there is only one ministry: the ongoing work of sharing the Good News about Jesus Christ. Of course, that "sharing" comes in many forms. If someone is hungry and their stomach is growling so loudly that they can't hear the words you are saying, should you start preaching to them? Of course not.

The church is central to God's plan for human beings. But remember that the church is more than just an organization. It is a living, breathing organism. You and I are God's church. When you give to biblical ministries, you are giving to the Lord. Just make sure that you do not neglect your local church. It takes money to keep those lights on so His light can be proclaimed.

Here are some tips for making informed choices:

- Avoid any "ministry" that does not acknowledge Jesus as Lord. Don't give them a dime or a second look. That doesn't mean that you should never give to a non-Christian. In those cases, you are the minister. Just be careful about inadvertently helping cultists or others who are opposed to the Lord of Glory.

- Determine whether they have a biblical statement of faith.

- Look for ministries who are accountable to a local church and/or a Christian body of directors.

- Make sure that they can show you exactly how the funds are to be used, and look closely at those records to see that they don't have an inappropriate amount going to administrative costs.

God doesn't want us to judge or condemn others. But we must be "fruit inspectors." If a ministry is asking you for money, but they have no biblical fruit to show for their efforts, go to another fruit stand.

Final thoughts: The ministries that you support don't have to have big numbers. It's just as crucial that you give to God-honoring work. Entrust your giving to people who trust in Christ and want to please Him. The more you give, the happier you'll be.

If you need additional ideas about what kinds of ministries need support, check out www.ecfa.org, a web site that introduces Christian givers to various ministries.

He has also called you to be a minister right where you are. Maybe you are in a position where God, through His people, wants to support the work that you are doing for His sake.

Day 34
WHAT DOES THE SAYING, "LET MONEY WORK FOR YOU" MEAN?

Most people work for money, meaning that they perform a service or provide a product and get money for it, and it's a short-term exchange. Financially successful people let money work for them, meaning that they know where to place and how to use their money so it grows, making it perform long-term.

If you are spending your money on things that don't last, e.g., entertainment, clothes, and expensive dinners, you are not putting your money to work. You'll begin to see money working for you, even while you sleep, when you have invested your money into giving, savings, and investments. And this is exactly what God wants you to do with the money He puts in your care.

One of the important principles here is to take advantage of compound interest. In a nutshell, compound interest is the nearly miraculous fact that your money can earn interest on the interest it's earning. This is when your money really works for you!

There are a few keys to enjoying the fruit of compound interest:

- The sooner you get started saving, the more amazing the results.

- The higher the interest rates, the better. Note: Generally, the higher the rate of return, the higher the risk. So measure your goals in that area.
- The more you can deposit, the more you will see in terms of returns.
- Don't touch those deposits! Taking money out of savings (before it's time) is like taking a half-baked brownie out of the oven. Don't do it. You'll kill the compound-interest effect.

Invest in savings as much as you can and as often as you can. You will be blown away at how compound interest will make more money from your money. This is one of the ways that the rich get richer.

Day 35
DO I NEED A FINANCIAL PLANNER?

A financial planner can be a valuable tool, but just as important as having an individual planner is having a plan. You plan where you're going to have lunch, where you will get your hair cut, even where you will be buried. Why would you not plan for how you will reach your financial goals?

Before you do that, though, the most important starting point is having a financial goal. In fact, have many of them. What is your giving goal? Your earnings goal? Your savings goal? Your retirement goal? Your vacation goal?

Here are some more tips about financial planning:

- Make sure that your plan is in writing.
- Make sure that you understand your plan and how to implement it.
- Make sure that you review and revise your plan frequently; I'd say at least two times a year.

I do indeed recommend that you work with a professional financial planner. Ask them for at least three references. If they can't give you the names of several people they have helped to make more, save more, and give away more, don't hire them. Some of the areas where a financial planner will help you are in determining what are good investments, how to make your money grow, and where to put it for the future.

Day 36
WHAT OTHER INVESMENTS SHOULD I CONSIDER?

Once you have your expenses covered and an appropriate amount in savings, it is good to consider investments to help grow your money. It might be a good idea to set up an IRA, especially if it's done through your employer. There are some real pluses to an IRA:

- The "miracle" of compound interest will multiply your savings.
- You get a significant write-off on your taxes.
- You can defer tax payments until you reach the maturation point.
- You can set up your fund so that deposits are made automatically.
- There are more aggressive ways to invest your money, but there are few ways that are more sure-fire or advantageous to beginning investors than an IRA savings plan.

Real estate has helped more people become well-to-do than any other single form of investment. Some of Robert Kiyosaki's books are helpful here. Kiyosaki is the author of *Rich Dad, Poor Dad* and several other excellent books. You can buy the "no money down" types of courses, but beware: Many of those are get-rich-quick schemes. And the only people who get rich quick from them are the infomercial creators.

You can invest in real estate funds, buy rental property, and invest in land. Start by buying your own home, and remember the three time-tested rules about real estate. Are you ready for them? Here they are: Location! Location! Location!

Historically, the stock market has been a good investment. But here are some tips for you if you decide to get into the market:

- Get in and stay in. Don't expect an immediate return.
- Diversify, diversify, and diversify.
- Look for long-term trends, and invest in funds or companies that have positioned themselves accordingly.

Supplies go down and prices go up. It looks like it will be that way for the foreseeable future. However, you also want to think long-term about things like alternative energy, the aging baby boomer population, etc. Make sure that you work with a professional broker. You can learn a lot and then venture out on your own. But make sure you have a good coach (financial advisor) before you step out onto this court.

Government bonds are as good as the government that prints them. Here in the US, this has been a good investment. Again, it's a long-term investment. You will get a better return than you would in a traditional bank account.

There are more aggressive ways to invest your money, but this may be a good place to start getting a higher yield on your savings. (Note: Municipal bonds are tax-free.)

Day 37
IF I GET A MORTGAGE, WHAT KINDS
OF TERMS ARE BEST?

Obviously, you want to get the lowest rate possible, though it is not always that simple. Look carefully at various home loan options. Read the fine print. If you don't understand it, find a professional who does, and have them explain it to you.

It's important to know that you are not just buying a house; you are buying a home loan. Here are some things to look out for:

- Don't get an adjustable rate.
- Avoid loans with prepayment penalties (this can affect your ability to refinance the loan later).
- The length of your loan—10, 20, 30, or 40 years— also makes a difference.

The interest rate matters, but also look at the big picture. What are you really buying into with this loan? Does it help your family to accomplish your goals? Will it help you solve your financial problems, or will it create bigger ones?

Also, the sooner you can pay off your mortgage, the better. There are some real advantages here:

- Your house payments are tax deductible.

- You can cut the length of your mortgage down— way down.
- You can have, and have access to, the full equity in your home.

If you can do this, go for it. You can accomplish this by starting with a shorter-term loan, but you can also do this with your current loan.

For example, if you have a thirty-year mortgage of $350,000 and your monthly payment is $2,200, and you pay an extra $500 per month toward the principal, you will pay off your loan almost eleven years early! And you will save more than $191,000 in interest.

A mortgage, in most cases, is the only way to get a home, but as long as you are wise about how much you finance and take care of this asset, it will be one of the best investments you will make.

Day 38

WHAT SHOULD I DO TO PREPARE FOR RETIREMENT?

You can count on death and taxes. And you can count on going to heaven if you have a personal relationship with God through Jesus Christ. But I wouldn't count on Social Security. We don't really know about the future of Social Security. There's nothing wrong with getting Social Security. You paid into it and you should be paid out from it. The problem is that we are now at the point where money is flowing out of Social Security at a faster rate than it is coming in.

It's probably best to think about it as dessert, and not as your main course. If it comes, that's nice, but if it doesn't, you won't go hungry. Depend on God, invest, and save wisely for your future. It's more likely that the government will take away than give in the future.

This is why it is important that you don't put off planning for retirement. Here's an acronym to help you plan ahead. You guessed it, the word is RETIRE:

Relax now. Don't wait until you're retired to rejuvenate your life. You can retire from stress by "casting all of your cares upon Him." While you are in this state of meditation and relaxation, the next step is...

Estimate your ideal retirement age. No one can do this for you. For some people this is fifty-five, for others it is eighty-five. The goal is to set the date when you want to retire, instead of being forced to work to manage your debt load or to pay for your standard of living.

Take stock of how much income you'll need at that age. This is a "best guesstimate," but you need to have an amount in mind.

Invest in a plan that will automatically pay you that monthly amount of income when you reach your ideal retirement age.

Regularly contribute to your savings and investment portfolio. Do this habitually, and you will ensure a secure retirement.

Enjoy your retirement, but don't check out of living. Use this opportunity to volunteer, spend time with your grandkids, or turn your hobby into a business. Have fun and be faithful.

Day 39
DO I NEED LIFE INSURANCE?

I used to think that you didn't need life insurance because you should "just trust God." And we do need to trust God, but we also need to be trustworthy servants for God. Look out for your family. God has promised you eternal life, but He has not told you how many days of earthly life you will have.

I recommend that you have at least a $500,000 policy of life insurance with your spouse as the main beneficiary (and director of your estate). But that's a base.

The rule of thumb that I like to use is: Take your annual income and multiply it by ten. If you currently make $50,000 per year, you need a $500,000 life insurance policy. If you are making $100,000 per year, take out a $1,000,000 life insurance policy. This is especially true if you are the sole or primary money- earner for your family. Remember that if you were to pass away unexpectedly, your family would have major costs, adjustments, taxes, and expenses to deal with.

Make sure that the policy will replace your income for more than just the first two or three years after you are gone. Again, I think that term life insurance is the best approach for this. You can shop for great term quotes online now.

Other types of insurance to consider to protect you and your family are:

- Car insurance: You may be required to have car insurance in your state or province. Whether you have to or not, get some. And have enough to cover the possibility that the guy who hits you may not have any insurance.

- Health insurance: If you can afford it, purchase health insurance with a high deductible. In the US, I prefer PPO to HMO because I want the freedom to choose the doctor or specialist who is right for me. Go to the doctor for regular check-ups, but avoid running up your medical bills just to meet your deductible. Remember, doctors are in business to make money. (The good ones also care about your health.)

- Business/Liability insurance: If you have a business, be sure to look into liability insurance. You can't afford to have one of your employees or vendors put you under because of negligence. I recommend at least a $1,000,000 liability policy to cover you and your business, even at the start-up level.

Some people may feel that insurance is a waste of money, but as they say, it is far better to have it and not need it than to need it and not have it.

Day 40
HOW CAN I LEAVE INCOME FOR MY CHILDREN
AFTER I DIE?

Giving your children an inheritance is a biblical idea, and you should plan ahead for it. If they are not adults yet, you should plan in your will or living trust to leave it with a designated beneficiary. This role should be given to someone you trust to look out for your kids.

Also, be careful about leaving too much money in the hands of your kids if they are young or still immature. You won't be doing them any favors if you give them more than they can handle or give it at the wrong time in their lives.

And remember the old Christian Latin expression: *"Memento mori."* This means, "Remember that you are mortal." Make your life on earth count, and think and pray ahead about what's best for your kids.

Think and plan these things through with your attorney. And remember that you should also plan ahead to support your church and other charities in your will. Plan on using term life insurance as the primary vehicle for leaving your kids with ongoing support.

If you want to create a will or a living trust yourself, there are forms available right in your local public library. You can also go to dozens of websites for help. (For example, check out: www.doyourownwill.com.

This is a resource you can access to get started online right away.) If you don't have a will, you really should get one. Even if you don't have much in the way of assets (yet), it is important that you leave clear-cut directions for your loved ones to follow. You can even handwrite a basic "Last Will and Testament" sheet. Sign it. Have a notary sign it. But in today's world, you really should have more than that.

Go over this important concern with your attorney. God has given you life. Be sure that you glorify Him when it's time to meet Him.

Dealing with Financial Burdens

"Ever notice that when you put the words 'THE' and 'IRS' together, it spells 'THEIRS'?"

—Jackie Mason

In Section 5 we will talk about some of the less pleasant parts of managing your money—paying off debt and dealing with the IRS. These two aspects of money matters are probably the most stress-inducing. The tips in this section will help to make things easier.

Day 41
WHAT IS THE FIRST STEP I CAN TAKE TO GAIN FINANCIAL INDEPENDENCE?

The first step of any journey begins with two questions:

- Where am I going?
- What's the best way to get there?

This applies to your financial life as well, so start by defining "financial independence." Does this mean that you never have to work a regular job again? Is it having one million dollars in the bank? Is it eliminating all of your debt?

Once you know the answers to those questions, you can work on mapping out the path to get there. This book has many tips, but one of the most important things that you can do to prepare for the journey is to begin by thanking God.

You should know that by the standards of human history, you already are rich. Did you know that? You will live longer, enjoy more material things, see more of the world, and enjoy better health than the richest of the rich who lived just a hundred years ago. So that's something huge to be grateful for.

Plus, you will enter heaven with all of your debts paid for in full by Jesus Christ (Isaiah 53:4-6).

Day 42
HOW CAN I DEAL WITH A MONEY CRISIS?

When someone asks me for help in dealing with a financial crisis, my first response might sound harsh, but I say it anyway. The best way is to not get into a money problem to begin with. I know that may seem obvious, but if you aren't actively making good decisions about money, you won't be equipped if something you can't control does happen.

But if you currently are facing a crisis and feeling hopeless, here's what I suggest:

- Give your problems to the One who can truly solve them, your Lord and Savior.
- Stop doing what you're doing and try a new approach. If you keep doing what you've been doing, you'll keep getting what you've been getting. Do at least one thing differently.
- Make a massive effort to do a "double and divide." This means, try to double the amount of work you do (not necessarily the hours, but the results you provide for others).

For example, if you are a salesperson and you make twenty outbound calls a day, start making forty. Also, take your expenses and divide them right in half. One half is the "would like to." The other half is the "have to."

Pay the "have to" items and hold off on all of the "would like to" items.

These steps won't necessarily solve your crisis, but they will help you to get redirected so that you can see a way out and make progress toward that goal.

Day 43
WHAT TOOLS CAN HELP ME FIX MY FINANCES?

There are several tips for securing a strong financial position. Many of those are things to do from the beginning, but that may not be possible if you find yourself in a hold, having never learned the right way to handle money. The following tools will help you to reverse course when things have gone wrong:

- Put God first and prioritize your giving!
- Keep a written record of every dollar that comes in and goes out.
- Stick with a budget that covers income, spending, savings, and debt reduction.
- Set aside a significant portion of your income for debt elimination, but don't pay down your debt so fast that you can't cover your basic living expenses. Create a specific debt repayment plan.
- Pay cash and stop borrowing. Remember: unsecured loans create an insecure future.

Day 44
HOW CAN I GET OUT OF DEBT?

Trying to get out of debt can feel so overwhelming. The most important thing that you can do is to stop adding to your debt. When you're in a hole... *stop* digging!

If you don't feel that you can trust yourself to manage your money well, consider having someone else handle your finances. That's right. Give your checkbook, all but one of your credit cards, and all of your bills to a bookkeeper. This might sound crazy at first. But take a look at the word accountant. It's where we get the word *accountable*.

You will likely find that you will spend less, save more, and watch your budget better when a professional is handling it with you. You're still in charge, and you need to meet with this person on a regular basis. But when they set a budget for you and give you an allowance, it won't be so easy to write a check or hit the ATM every time you feel the urge.

Create a step-by-step, get-out-of-debt plan with your CPA, credit counselor, or bookkeeper. Be optimistic, but realistic. It probably took you ten to fifteen years or more to pile on that debt. Try to make at least a three-year plan that you are accountable for following that will have you debt-free, except for your house and car. It can be done. And you are more likely to do it if you have a financial professional holding you to it.

Day 45
HOW SOON CAN I BE DEBT-FREE?

Have you noticed that when you work on a deadline, a deadline works on you? It's true. The best predictor of when you'll be out of debt is the one you make. Set a goal.

But it is important to set an optimistic, yet realistic, goal for your debt-free date with destiny. If your debt load is over $10,000, you might have a two-year time frame. It all depends on your income level and necessary expenses.

You can buy computer programs that will take all of your debt data, along with your debt repayment schedule, and spit out an exact time frame that you can count on if you stay on schedule. If you get behind, don't get down on yourself. Keep your head up and keep after it. You didn't get into debt overnight. Give yourself time (and grace) to get out. You can do it. "Owe nothing to anyone except to love one another" (Romans 13:8 NASB).

Day 46
SHOULD I CUT UP ALL OF MY CREDIT CARDS?

Grab those scissors and snip away! In our world today, you may really need one credit card for emergencies, as a form of ID, and as a convenience when you
don't have a checkbook with you. But I would still advise you to cut up all of your credit cards, except for the
following:

- A simple, low-interest, low credit limit card. The
  higher the limit, the more tempted you are to
  run up a balance you can't pay off. You don't really need the "silver" or "platinum" card, etc. You
  may find that the benefits are not worth the extra money.

- American Express. Why? Because you have to
  pay it off at the end of each month. Plus, there's
  no interest on the basic green card. (Avoid their
  Optima card. It is just like the other high-inter-
  est credit cards.)

- A bank ATM/check debit card. These now come
  with a VISA or MasterCard logo on them so you
  can use them for purchases. But the helpful
  thing is that the money is taken right from your
  checking account. That might not feel nice at the
  moment, but it sure beats the credit card trap of
  high interest rates and the pain of debt.

If you have credit cards other than these, stop using them immediately, close the accounts so you won't be tempted to use them, and make a reasonable plan for paying off the balances.

Day 47
SHOULD I STOP SAVING OR GIVING WHEN I AM IN DEBT?

In a real sense, when you pay down your debt, you are saving money on high interest rates, late fees, and more. But Curt Whipple has another perspective in his book, *You Will Never Have Financial Freedom by Paying Off Your Debt* (you can order it on Amazon.com). Whipple's main idea is that you have to do both—save and pay off debt. If you only focus on paying down your debt, it's like you are eliminating a negative without building a positive (net worth).

What I recommend to my clients and friends is the "5 & 5" plan. Take that 10% that you are saving and split it into two parts. Use half of it for debt reduction and the other half for savings. For my really motivated clients, I recommend the "10 & 10" plan. This one will have you financially independent in a very short period. Save/invest 10% of your income, and reduce your debt with 10% of your income.

Wow! This means that you are living on just 70% of your income. You may think, *Wait, that doesn't add up!* But remember, you put God (and giving to His work) as number one. This means that you set aside 10% or more right off the top for Him. I have seen God bless this plan time and again for those who trust Him.

In fact, I believe that one of the reasons you hardly have enough may be because you aren't giving to God and others. And please note that you can give in many ways. Give of your time. Give of your expertise. Give of your possessions. Give someone a listening ear. There was a time in my life when I was unemployed. My wife and I agreed to continue giving to our church, and the Lord blessed us because of that. Within seven months, God enabled me to start my own tax accounting practice. Today, we have more than 3,500 clients.

Too many people wait till they "have enough" before they start giving. The problem is, when is enough ever really enough? When Rockefeller was the richest man in the world, somebody once asked him, "How much money do you need, Mr. Rockefeller?" He answered, "A little more."

So hand it over. Not just your money. Hand over your heart, mind, soul, and strength to God. Watch and see. God will bless you. He will give you the ability to have and to give even more.

Day 48
HOW CAN I SAVE MONEY ON MY TAXES?

It's not as hard as you think to cut down your tax responsibility. Here are some ABCs to guide you:

Accounting is key. Keep track of every dollar you spend and every dollar you make.

Be sure you stay current with the IRS. Pay your taxes on time. You don't want to get behind and have to deal with late payments, fees, or the dreaded liens on your property, bank levies, or wage garnishments.

Count every deduction you possibly can. It's wrong to not pay taxes (both biblically and legally), but it is poor stewardship to not look for every deduction that you are entitled to take.

Some of the tax breaks you may be missing out on are:

• Health-care benefits. You shouldn't pay this tax when your employer pays the premiums for your health insurance and health care.

• Contributions to retirement accounts.

• Lower rates on dividends and long-term capital gains.

• The mortgage-interest deduction.

- State and local income taxes and personal property taxes.
- Charitable contributions.
- Children under age seventeen. The child tax credit puts $1,100 per child in your pocket.
- The Earned Income Tax Credit. You may qualify for this tax credit, which is targeted at low-income taxpayers.
- Life insurance or annuity contracts. There is no current tax on the inside investment income.

If you are self-employed or own your own business, you are likely in a position to qualify for many other tax breaks. As always, discuss this with your tax professional.

Day 49
DO I NEED A CPA?

I highly recommend that you get a CPA to help you with tax preparation. Of course, I am biased because I am a CPA. (Go to the back of this book to find out how to contact my office and for additional resources.)

A CPA is a Certified Public Accountant. This means that they are qualified to advise you in terms of your money, the tax codes, and proper reporting procedures. There is a wonderful saying: "Success leaves clues." Most financially successful people have a CPA on their team.

Chances are very good that your CPA will pay for himself or herself several times over in terms of helping you to save money on your taxes, handling your tax planning, and by advising you on "money matters."

Read those last two words above one more time: money matters. That's why it's important to have a professional CPA helping you to make every dollar count!

Other than that, there are many ways to file your tax returns. You can do it via the mail, and now even with the convenience of the internet.

Again, the important thing is that you file on time, and file properly. If you do not have a CPA, you should at the very least file your taxes with a certified tax preparer.

You've heard the saying, "It takes money to make money," right? Well, this is also true with your taxes. You might say, "It takes money to save money." So I want to recommend that you hire a successful tax preparer. It will cost you more than doing it yourself or at a small-based firm, but you will see the difference in the savings you get in terms of your higher deductions and lower tax liabilities.

Day 50
HOW DO I DEAL WITH THE IRS?

The first rule is: never ignore the IRS. If you have a problem, trust me (I am an IRS problem solver), it will not go away by itself.

Some things to start doing:

1. Hire an expert to help you. Go to www.YourIR-SProblemSolvers.com, for starters.

2. Make a payment plan with the IRS and start making payments on time, every time.

3. Consider doing an "offer and compromise" with the IRS.

4. Don't be intimidated by the IRS. This is a branch of the government, but remember that government is "for the people." If you cooperate with them, you will get better results than you will by avoiding, covering up, or running from your problems.

5. Be ethically aggressive. For example, did you know that you can amend your tax returns for the previous three years?

It's quite likely that you may have overpaid or understated your deductions on previous tax returns. You can file amended returns for previous years. One of my clients recently did this and saved $15,000 on his IRS bill.

Yes, in many cases the IRS will work with you. Ask for a payment plan, and if you run into problems, you can often set up a payment plan called an installment agreement to get caught up.

But please keep in mind:

- You want to have an installment agreement from the IRS. This is your go-ahead to make those payments. It's a contractual agreement you make with the IRS.
- You will likely have to pay extra in penalties and interest. Usually, these are fairly reasonable. But if you can pay in full, it's best to do so.
- If you default on your payment plan, you can be in worse shape than when you started. Keep on top of it, and stay in close communication with the IRS.

The worst thing that you can do is to get frustrated with the government and cheat on your taxes.

How do we know that it is wrong? Because God says, "You shall not steal" (Exodus 20:15 NIV), and cheating the government is stealing. He did not qualify that with "except from organizations that frustrate you."

Be aggressive on your tax returns, but be honest. Take advantage of tax avoidance, not tax evasion. Report your income. Make sure that your tax deductions are legitimate.

You may get audited at some point (keep your records for seven years). As a matter of fact, you will get audited by a much higher authority than the IRS. God, Himself, will ask you to give an account of how you managed His money.

Growing Your Business and Your Money

"The only thing that stands between a man and what he wants in life is often merely the will to try it and the faith to believe that it is possible."
—David Viscott

In Section 6, we will look at ways to increase your earning potential, expand your business opportunities, and protect your assets. The information here addresses the practical aspects of starting a business, how best to improve your work situation, and much more.

Day 51
HOW CAN I EARN MORE MONEY?

Here's a modern business term based on a biblical idea: create value. This means that you will be paid in direct proportion to the specific contribution you make to your company or to your customers. If you are serious about making more, you have to do more, serve more, and work smarter. Grow your company's reputation and profits.

Maybe you want to start your own full- or part-time business. The truth is, nothing happens in the economy until somebody sells something to somebody else. Being able to identify what the marketplace needs, and how you might be able to provide that, is the key to success in business. What can you sell that is of service to others? Your expertise? Your labor? Your technology? Your new way of doing something that saves time and money?

There's a famous motivational book called Think and Grow Rich by Napoleon Hill. Some people want the rich part without having to do the thinking part. Think about how you can contribute to others, and don't be afraid to charge them a fair price for it. There's nothing wrong with that.

Obviously, that's easier to do if you own your own business. But you can have this mentality even as an employee. Here are the two things you need to do:

- Do more than what you are paid for. Don't expect people to pay you more for doing or delivering less. This is where some people make a mistake. Provide a greater value or service than you do now.

- Communicate to your customers or boss; educate them about the great service you are rendering for them. They may not be aware of how much you are helping them, saving them, or contributing to their well-being. So tell them.

Day 52
HOW CAN I GIVE MYSELF A
PROMOTION OR A RAISE?

First, I want to answer this question on a personal level. "When you praise, you get a raise!" This means that your attitude truly does determine your altitude in life. Try it. Praise God and see if you can be depressed at the same time. It's impossible. But I know that we are talking about a financial raise, so here are some tips:

- Raise your level of commitment and service to your employer.
- Raise the number of hours you are working.
- Raise your level of responsibility and become a go-to team player.
- Raise your level of expertise by attending a training course or developing a new skill.
- Raise the value you bring to your company.

And, finally, ask for a raise. That's your part. But make your request in the context of your contribution. Don't say, "Hey, can I have a raise?" Instead, say, "Boss, I am so glad to work here. I want you to know that I am making a real effort to help you grow this company. In the last six months, I have improved our computer systems, increased our sales by X amount of money, and saved us a bunch of money. I estimate that I have earned or saved our company X amount this year. With this in mind, I am asking for an X amount increase in my annual salary." Your employer will respect you for asking when you connect your request to your contribution.

The same is true when asking for a promotion. Here's an acronym that will help you get a promotion. It's built on the word GROW:

Give your company your very best. Ask your supervisor(s) for brutally honest feedback about the results you have been creating for the company.

Response-ability: Accept full responsibility for your actions. And if you are a team leader, be willing to take the responsibility for your team's results, too—even if a problem occurred that's not your fault. Also, learn to be responsive. If your organization is going through a crisis or a unique opportunity, respond (and help) accordingly.

Offer to expand what you do for the company in exchange for an increase in pay and/or a portion of the new revenue you create. What small business owner wouldn't welcome an employee saying, "If I can bring additional business to the firm, can I have a percentage of it?"

Welcome feedback. Invite input from your bosses and co-workers.

Try to separate who you are as a person (remember that you are made in God's image and fully accepted in Christ) from what you do in the world of bottom-line results. Listen and look for ways that you can improve your contribution to the company.

If you are willing to GROW personally, your income will grow too. You can't increase your value—for long—without increasing your income. It's one of God's laws. Keep sowing and you will reap.

Day 53
HOW CAN I EARN MORE WITHOUT SACRIFICING QUALITY FAMILY TIME?

There's a lot of talk these days about "working smarter, not harder." Who says you can't do both? God worked six days and rested one. We tend to work four and a half days and goof off for two and a half.

Do I think that you should cut into quality time with your husband or wife or kids? No. I have worked twenty years of extended hours from January to April 15th, which we affectionately call "tax season." This is a very demanding time, yet my family tells me they didn't feel that they were disregarded or neglected, because I purposed that they were a priority and scheduled quality time with them. Establish regular times with your spouse or children. Make sure that God and your family are priorities in your life.

Cut out several time wasters. Let's be honest here. You, like most North Americans, probably watch TV for a minimum of ten hours a week. Minimum. Am I right?

What if you used those ten-plus hours to make your hobby a part-time job, to write that book you've been meaning to write, to work at that restaurant a couple of nights a week, or to address envelopes?

What if you went to bed thirty minutes earlier each night, and got to work 30 minutes sooner? You'd probably feel better, work better, and increase your income.

You have exactly all the time there is. The question is: How are you using it? Eliminate one or two unproductive things in your life and find ways to increase your income in that time you save.

Hollywood usually is not a good place to look for examples, but some Hollywood executives who started out in the mailroom and ended up in the boardroom are good examples in terms of their dedication at the office. Many of them started out by being the first one in the door and the last one out.

More important than how many hours you work is how many valuable results you are creating for your organization. Be sure to spend 80% of your time on the 20% of your job that contributes the most to the bottom line and well-being of your company.

What would happen if you were the first one in (or you arrived a half hour earlier than normal)? Try it for four weeks and see what happens. Your boss might have a heart attack... or your boss might give you a raise.

Day 54
SHOULD I STAY AT A JOB WHERE I HAVE WORKPLACE CONFLICTS?

Leo Tolstoy wrote: "Everyone thinks of changing the world, but no one thinks of changing himself."

Have you noticed yet that you can't change other people? It's a hard lesson, but the sooner we learn it, the better off we are. It's also nearly impossible to change yourself, but with God's help, you can.

How does this relate to your job? Simple. When you make changes in your attitude about the job, about your boss or coworkers, and about your own work, you will notice that things will change. They have to. It's a scientific law that for every action (your improved attitude) there is a reaction (from your associates, customers, etc.).

Maybe you can tap into a little competitive spirit here. That's right. But do it God's way. Are your co-workers driving you nuts? Try:

- out-serving them;
- out-working them;
- out-caring for them.

You will possibly win them over, and you will certainly impress your supervisors. Here's the crucial thing: You cannot expect anything from them (but more whining). And remember, you might work with them, but you don't work for them—you work for God, so act like it. God didn't put you into your work environment by mistake. Do your best to make the best of it.

As Jesus said, "Let your good deeds shine out for all to see, so that everyone will praise your heavenly Father" (Matthew 5:16 NLT).

Day 55
HOW DO I KNOW WHEN CHANGING JOBS IS THE RIGHT DECISION?

The first thing to change about your current job is your attitude. Ask yourself how you can bring more excellence and enthusiasm to it.

But there is nothing wrong with changing jobs for the right reasons. Here are a few of them.

Change jobs when...

• you are currently being asked to do something illegal or immoral;

- you cannot provide for yourself or your family in your current position;
- you have a clear opportunity to make more income and make a bigger difference for God's kingdom with a different job;
- God is calling you to a whole new line of work, such as owning your own business or working in a full-time ministry position.

Maybe you want to leave your job and work from home. Here are a few pros and cons to consider.

PROS
- The commute is nice!
- You can work in your pajamas (though that is not recommended).

- You can write off many of your expenses on your taxes.
- You may have more time for work and family.

CONS

- You run the (very likely) risk of being constantly distracted by kids, the mail, noise, visitors, etc.
- You will have a harder time attracting professional employees, and you may limit your growth potential.
- The impression you give your customers may be "amateur". And that's not good at all. When you have a separate place of business, your attitude and credibility in the work arena will likely be strengthened.

Regardless of what change you are considering, pray and ask God for direction. Ask Him to specifically confirm the best direction to you by opening doors or by closing doors. God is more ready to guide us than we realize. He says that He will guide us and instruct us in the way that we are to go; that He will guide us by His eye (Psalm 32:8). Do you remember when you were young how your parents guided you by "the look"—no words needed? We knew their directives, exactly. We also knew their look of pleasure and affirmation upon us.

Day 56
WHAT DO I NEED TO KNOW ABOUT STARTING MY OWN BUSINESS?

Maybe you have heard about the book Do What You Love and the Money Will Follow by Marsha Sinetar. What a great line. And it's true. If you do what you love, you'll never "work" another day in your life. That is why many people want to start their own business.

If you are going to go this route, it is crucial that you do something that you have a passion for. I tell my employees that you've got to love what you are doing or start looking for something else. Work is such an adventure when you are passionate about what you are doing.

Once you've identified that passion, use these ideas to move forward:

- Have a vision and be able to cast it to others.
- Set your business up so that it's purpose-driven and provides service beyond your customers' expectations.
- Work on your business, not in it.
- Set your business up so that it's process-driven, not personality-driven.
- Create operating procedures for everything that you do.

All of this presupposes one important thing: You must bring a valuable product or service to people. I happen to do taxes and accounting because it is the best avenue for me to fulfill my passion, which is helping people.

And just as importantly, you must do a super job of marketing your business. Read as many marketing books as you can. The DISC personality test is a good indicator of the type of business, or position within a business, for you. It's fun and easy to take.

Find the type of work or business that connects to your God-given strengths. God has designed you to prosper in the gifts and talents that He has given to you.

These days, many businesses are internet-based. These five tips will help you to make your venture a success. You will need a:

- distinctive product or service,
- domain name that reflects that brand,
- delivery system where your customers can access your product or service,
- descriptive website,
- detailed operational system. Think of your website as an online brochure. It's very important that you make it clear to browsers how you can help them right now.

If you have a vision for a new business, go for it. Write out exactly what it will take to not only conceive it, but also to manage and operate your business. Have a plan.

Day 57
HOW SHOULD I STRUCTURE MY BUSINESS?

If you work freelance, have a DBA ("doing business as") license, do consulting work, or do anything else where you set your own hours and fees, there are advantages to being self-employed. This is also called a "sole proprietorship." It means that you are the boss, the owner of the business. The main advantage is that you will have a tremendous opportunity for tax deductions, also happily referred to as write-offs. You might be surprised by how many of your expenses are tax deductible when you are self-employed.

However, there is also an upside to incorporating your business. One of the main advantages is that you will have a legal "shield" that can protect your personal finances from lawsuits. The law treats a corporation as an entity of its own, almost like a person.

You have several choices if you incorporate. You can become:

- An LLC – this is a Limited Liability Company.
- An "S" Corp – this is often appropriate for a mid-sized company with an owner(s) highly active in the business.
- A "C" Corp – this offers the most protection and is generally for the larger companies, or a company intending to become much larger.

Another possibility is a franchise business, i.e., a Subway, KFC, or UPS store. With these options, all of the business "bugs" have been worked out of the system. Your main concern becomes operating their proven, winning formula. A few notes:

- 90% of new businesses fail in their first year of operation. The number is much lower for franchise businesses.
- If you are a pioneering, visionary person, a franchise business may not be right for you, unless you want to become a franchisor (like Ray Kroc was with McDonald's).
- If you buy a franchise business, you will really be in the management business. Your biggest challenge will be hiring and training the right people to run the show. The good news is that most franchisors do a good job of preparing you for this.

Besides franchising, you may also want to look at licensing and, believe it or not, some multi-level businesses (the legal ones), because your initial investment may be considerably less, and you may have more freedom and flexibility than in a franchise system. There are many options for entrepreneurship. Just be sure to speak with a professional about your situation and what is best for you. A business or tax attorney can advise you and can also help you to file appropriately.

Day 58
HOW DO I FIND START-UP MONEY?

The best way to find start-up money is to save for it. This way you are not indebted to a rich uncle or to the government. Finding the money is not your biggest problem. There are hundreds of companies hoping you'll borrow their money. They will make back thousands and thousands more than they loan you.

Your real challenge is in knowing how best to use that money, and a business plan will help you to do that. Here is why a business plan is a great thing:

- First, it will tell you whether you have a viable business.
- Second, you can use it to attract a business partner or investors.
- Third, it will give you a blueprint for operating your business.

One more thought. You may not need as much seed money as you think. If you use low cost/high response forms of advertising, i.e., word of mouth, referrals, and the internet, you may be able to finance your way as you go.

Along with your business plan, you will need financial statements. These can be drawn up in various ways.

One of the best ones is called a "P & L." This simply stands for a profit and loss statement.

You should learn how to read these, and also learn how to create them for your personal and business finances. It's sort of like getting your blood pressure taken. You need to look carefully at:

1. How much money is coming in?
2. How much money is going out?
3. What is the difference between these two?

If your blood pressure is unhealthy, you adjust your diet and exercise. If your money situation is not healthy, you need to make adjustments in your budget, your income, and your necessary expenses.

One final note: the best avenue to having start-up money is to get started and to make certain that you are providing the most excellent service possible. The greatest momentum that can be developed for the most growth is to have happy clients who feel cared for and valued. The greatest growth that I have experienced as a CPA has come through referrals.

Day 59

HOW CAN I GROW THE BUSINESS I ALREADY OWN?

There are hundreds of ways to grow your existing business. However, foundationally speaking, the core is found in your client service philosophy. Always keep this in mind: the way that you build your business grows out of your conviction of what separates you from the rest, in your products and in your service.

Practically speaking, here are three main thoughts to follow in growing your business. Marketing wizard Jay Abraham's ideas are helpful. You can:

- Target more customers. Understand the value of a customer, and determine the value of their patronage. How often do they buy from you? How much do they normally spend? How long do they stay with your business? For example, if your average customer sale is $300, and your typical customer buys three times a year, you earn $900 annually from your average customer. This means that an average customer contributes $4,500 to your gross earnings over a five-year period. Just ten more customers would result in a $45,000 increase in sales over five years.

- Increase the value/price of what you are selling. What would happen if you increased your price by just 10%? The key to increasing your fees or prices is to simultaneously increase the value that you are delivering to your customers. Today's customer is more value-conscious than ever before.

- Increase the number of purchases that your customers make with you. If your customers were to buy from you four times a year instead of just three, that would have a significant impact on your annual income.[3]

Here's where it gets really exciting. If you can increase each of these areas by just a 10% increment, and that is very attainable, your business will grow 30%.

Day 60
HOW CAN I AVOID LAWSUITS?

The Scripture is very helpful here. It says, "Do all that you can to live in peace with everyone" (Romans 12:18 NLT).

If your issue is with a fellow believer in Christ, you should avoid suing. The New Testament is very clear about this. First, since you share the same Lord, you can work it out. Second, you need to be a good witness to the unbelieving world.

Check out Matthew 18:15-17, in which Jesus instructs us about dealing with conflict:

- Go to your brother or sister privately and directly.
- If they won't listen to you, take another believer along with you.
- If they still won't listen, take it to the church, i.e., the elders or the church leadership.

If the person still won't listen, seek counsel—which might ultimately lead to court, but this should not be your goal. Try prayer. Try mediation. Try arbitration. Do all that you can to avoid court. If you are being attacked in court, you must go on the defensive; even the Apostle Paul defended his rights in court as a Roman citizen. Look out for your family, business, and reputation. If someone is threatening to sue you, listen to him or her. Let them blow off some steam. Many times, they just want to be heard. If you have wronged them, make it right.

I believe that the same principles are true for dealing with non-believers. But we need to be especially on the lookout when it comes to our brothers and sisters in Christ. So, if you have a dispute with a nonbeliever, try to settle it directly, and then through a mediator; finally, try legal arbitration. If none of these things is effective, a legal suit may be your only recourse.

Conclusion

I pray that over the last sixty days you have learned a lot about yourself and your relationship to money, and that you have grown in your relationship with God.

During each of the six sections we:

- looked at what the Bible says about money,
- discovered how money affects your life,
- learned about managing what God blesses you with,
- explored how to make your money work for you,
- discussed the best ways to deal with financial burdens, and
- considered many possibilities for growth within your job or a new one.

The tips I have provided are based in biblical teaching and practical experience, and I believe they will make a difference in your financial future.

If you have further questions, please see the contact information in the back of the book. If you would like to go deeper into this study, get our workbook as a companion study.

Acknowledgements

God has enriched my life with so many wonderful relationships. These people have been God's love and faithfulness extended to me, and I want to take this opportunity to acknowledge them as a tremendous source of encouragement and strength:

I am eternally grateful to my precious wife, Dana. She has faithfully and selflessly given her love and support to champion me to become all that I can be, in every area of my life. Our Lord has truly blessed me with an amazing wife, whom I love very much. Our life verse is: "Trust in the Lord with all your heart, and lean not on your own understanding; in all your ways acknowledge Him, and He shall direct your paths" (Proverbs 3:5-6 NKJV). I am truly blessed that God has directed our paths to be joined together.

My overwhelming and abounding appreciation for my precious daughters, Lisa and Marci, who are the loves of my life and who have a wonderful way of keeping me young! Being their dad has been one of the greatest privileges and joys of my life.

My wonderful parents, Mario and Celeste, who have always encouraged me to pursue personal and professional excellence.

My pastors: to my former pastor, Dr. Paul Risser, who instilled the biblical principles of stewardship and giving into my life through his teachings, example, and personal counsel; and to Pastor Matthew Barnett, whose friendship and pastoral care have been priceless to me. My brothers in Christ: George, Bob, and Bill, who meet with me every Friday morning for fellowship, prayer, Bible study, and accountability. These men have been an anchor of support to me.

My committed staff, on which I depend daily. I value and appreciate their dedication to excellence in partnering with me as we serve our clients together.

Suggested Reading

"Today a reader, tomorrow a leader."

—W. FUSSELMAN

Here are some great books that I recommend for further reading. You'll notice that several of these are old spiritual classics:

• *The Autobiography of George Muller*, by George Muller. Read this amazing story and see how God loves to provide for His children and the miracles that take place when you trust Him with all of your needs.

• *Hudson Taylor's Spiritual Secret*, by Howard Taylor. This book will knock your socks off about the power of prayer and God's desire to give and to bless those who give.

• *Secrets of the Vine*, by Bruce Wilkinson. Bruce is a terrific Bible teacher. Don't miss this message about God's abundant love and our need to connect deeply to Him.

• *The Richest Man in Babylon,* by George Clason. Before The Automatic Millionaire, and before the hundreds of other personal finance books, Clason wrote this wonderful fable over seventy years ago. The lessons about earning, saving, and debt reduction are still valid today.

• *A Currency of Hope.* This book, published by Debtors Anonymous, offers a proven program for recovery from debt and compulsive spending, based on the 12-step programs.

Another important book to purchase is a personal journal. Make notes about your dreams and goals. Keep track of your giving, your earnings, and your savings, and how God is answering your prayers. Watch how God blesses your life and finances when you put Him first!

About Liberatore Accounting Services

"Our goal is to free you to focus on what's truly important in your life."

Philip L. Liberatore, Certified Public Accountant, is a Southern California-based professional corporation providing accounting, consulting, and tax preparation services to businesses and individuals. The firm offers a full range of financial services and solutions with a revolutionary approach: "We listen to our clients." For more information, please visit our website:

www.LiberatoreCPA.com

PHILIP L. LIBERATORE, CPA

A Note From IRS Problem Solvers, Inc.

"Stop IRS pain and get your life back!"

The only sure thing about IRS problems is that they don't go away by themselves. If you are suffering from the intense financial pain and psychological pressure that an IRS problem can inflict, IRS Problem Solvers can help. We care about your problem and can offer you expert solutions. Our specialists represent over 125 years of experience in resolving tax issues including audits, federal tax levies, wage garnishment, liens, and more.

Call 1-877-6-SOLVER, or visit

www.YourIRSProblemSolvers.com

PHILIP L. LIBERATORE, CPA

About *God, Money, & You*

"Give more. Make more. Save more."

Put God first. Start giving and start living! Integrate your spiritual and financial lives by learning and practicing God-centered principles for your life and your money.

Sign up for our free email newsletter packed with valuable tips, resources, life-changing stories, and more tools for transformation.

www.LiberatoreCPA.com

Endnotes

1. Earl Nightingale, *The Strangest Secret*

2. Robert Kiyosaki, *Rich Dad, Poor Dad*

3. Jay Abraham, pg. 107

https://www.youtube.com/watch?v=cvSGC8rpfMU